Introduction

Red is one of the three primary colours. Mixed with blue it becomes purple and with yellow it makes orange plus many variations between depending on the proportions of each colour mixed together. With the addition of black and white to create shades and tints an enormous choice can be assembled.

Within the colour circle, the opposite and complementary colour to red is green.

In many of the sketches and samples shown, green is evident and acts as a foil to highlight and show red to great advantage. Equal amounts of the two colours can result in a pulsating effect as often seen on Christmas wrapping paper. The other primary colours of yellow and blue are complementary to purple and orange respectively.

Positive and negative symbolism

Using this colour as a main focus has been an fascinating journey and our awareness has been greatly intensified. Most of us appreciate the symbolism of rolling out the red carpet for important visitors, a full-bodied red wine to nourish and Robin redbreast personifying Christmas. Regal red velvets, sumptuous silks and satins can suggest festive seasons or celebration days such as the exotic red and golden saris worn by a bride at a traditional Indian wedding. An excess of red holly berries can warn us of a severe winter to come as well as being part of 'decking the boughs with holly and ivy'. In contrast, red, the colour of blood, red flag to alert some danger or a red card given to a player on a football pitch for bad behaviour offer less comforting aspects.

The emotional response to the colour red can be quite diverse. On one hand it can suggest warmth, passion, intimacy and love. Red roses, hearts and the celebration of St. Valentine's Day foster these responses. In contrast, red signs can alert us to caution, a number of hazards and danger.

The red ' family' of colours can range from sumptuous, hot pinks suggesting sunshine and fiesta through to softer, toning maroon hues observed when looking at branches of leafless tress in winter. Observations can include succulent bright scarlet, strawberries, pinky, lilac raspberries, the shiny crimson skins of dragon fruit through to the deep, dark, rich hues of ripe plums, cherries and aubergines. The very description of the colour can activate ones taste buds. Is it the colour and texture together with the association with summer, relaxation and halcyon days that intrigue, comfort and nurture?

Looking through 'rose coloured glasses' and ' in the pink' are feel good sayings where as 'bloodshot' or 'in the red' or being in debt, have negative

connotations. Less attractive associations can be 'lust', 'the scarlet woman', 'red light district' and the distressing aspects of fire, blood, torture and death. The red planet Mars is often named God of War. Bold, aggressive behaviour is at times described as 'seeing red' and people with red hair it is assumed have fiery tempers. Images of angry people in cartoons or on seaside postcards are often depicted in tones of this colour.

Danger, no entry, traffic lights and stop signs displayed in red, immediately alert us to possible hazards ahead and give straightforward, urgent communications to most societies.

Above: *A sketch of red onions painted with Koh- I-Noor and gouache paints.*

Inside front cover: *A selection of silk, cotton, wool, hemp, and synthetic threads celebrating the fabulous range of yarns now available.*

Car lights!

During the process of seeking out fresh approaches to the chosen subject of red, car lights became a focus. We have all suffered traffic jams at one time or another and despaired at the lines of red taillights ahead stretching as far as the eye can see. Photographs of cars moving in the dark have resulted in some spectacular images showing continuous networks or elegant swirls of red lines.

On closer inspection, it is amazing how varied the actual lights are in size and shape. Square, rectangular, circular forms manufactured in glass, plastic and chrome offer a diversity of interesting patterns. The grid structures within show some exciting effects. If brake and indicator lights are added to the general cluster, the reflections one on another combine to make unexpected patterns. These could suggest great potential for unusual design developments.

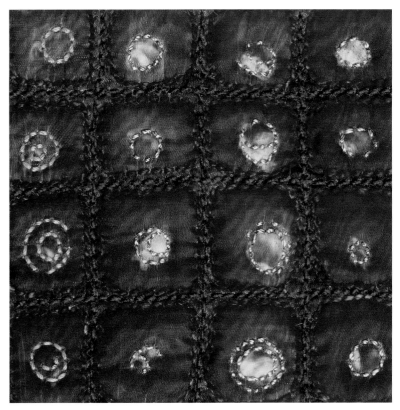

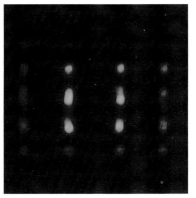

Above: Photographs of a variety of car lights JB.

Left: A simple pattern was painted onto paper with transfer paints before being transferred by ironing on to a shiny synthetic fabric. (Transfer to Transform, Book 4). This was placed on top of a layer of cotton muslins and wadding (batting) in order to quilt the design. Backstitches worked in bold silk and linen threads outlined the shapes.

Right: Red felt was placed beneath a woollen fabric and the embellishing machine was used to draw and build up the grid arrangement working on both sides. Small pieces of velvet and layers of red and orange wool tops were embellished to highlight brighter elements of the design.

Cut through sections, seed chambers and views from different angles provide excellent starting points for pattern and exploration.

Once the initial studies have been made they may be used for a wide range of pattern making methods.

Colour schemes torn from magazine paper, if carefully selected, provide a palette of rich and subtle variations of red.

Lino printing, although a traditional technique, is still a very effective way of producing a printing block that works well on fabric and paper. The tools and materials are available in most art shops. Begin by drawing or tracing the design on the surface of the lino before cutting away the negative or positive shape. The cutting takes time but is well worth the effort as the resulting block is almost indestructible. The only drawback to the technique is that injuries can be

Pomegranates and patterns

When drawing any fruit it helps to get to know the subject by looking at all aspects of it from different angles before making initial exploratory studies.

The pomegranate oozes juicy voluptuousness and can be an exciting source of inspiration.

It has associations with ancient symbolism and some believe it was the original 'forbidden fruit' in The Garden of Eden rather than an apple and in the Middle Ages it was known as pomuni granatum or seeded apple.

A close look will reveal that the tough outer skin is pocked and textured and displays a fantastic assortment of pinks, reds, ochres and deep maroons with hints of burnt orange.

When cut open the dark red seeds are enclosed in a rosy coloured jelly like substance.

Throughout history there are examples of its use in designs on textiles and interiors.

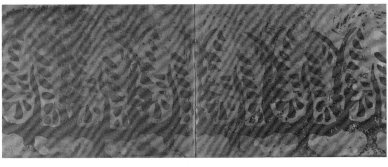

sustained if the enthusiasm of the cutting away makes people forget that the cutting tool must be worked away from the hand and not towards it.

The lino block may be used with fabric paints onto cloth or with printing inks onto paper.

Acrylic paints can also work well on paper and fabric.

It is best to apply the colouring media with a sponge or roller for even distribution.

The prints can be formally registered or randomly placed and overprinted with contrasting colour shifts. Lino blocks could also be used for other printing and discharging effects to make complex patterned surfaces.

Left: The illustration shows the materials and the finished block with some sketchbook trials and cloths that have been printed.

Right: This sample features a sheer synthetic surface layer printed with the 'pomegranate block' and then applied to another fabric before fusing with an embellishing machine.

The red velvet seeds were bonded to the surface before being embellished.

There are many ways in which such cloths could be further enriched with quilting or hand and machine stitching.

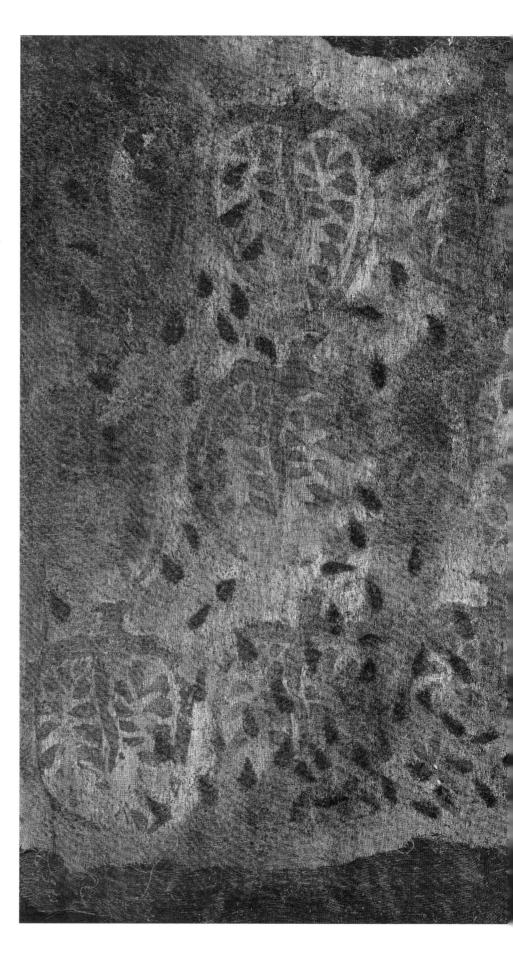

Peeling paint

The 'Lutradur' was first painted with acrylic paints and then a layer of painted 'Bondaweb' ironed over it to make a rich and robust surface. The image was further built up with 'Lutradur' shapes bonded together. Metallic effects were achieved by ironing gold printing foil onto the bonded surface (see Bonding and Beyond, Book 3) and the use of metallic effect surface paints.

Turquoise and red sheer nylon scarves were ironed over the built up layers and surfaces before being distressed with the application of a heat tool. Careful directed use of this tool can enhance the drawing qualities of a stitched piece.

Simple hand and machine stitching that echoed the boat structure completed the piece.

The old decaying boat seen here was beached on a sandy patch of ground surrounded by the sun-scorched landscape on the Greek island of Samos.

The effect of the erosion by salty sea spray and fierce sun has etched the glass fibre into a fragile lace-like texture.

The peeling paint has revealed layers of colour and texture with dynamic red blue contrasts.

Holiday sketchbooks are a constant reference, far more so than photographs, because they are a personal record. The effort of standing still, looking carefully and attempting to record the information as honestly as possible leaves a much more powerful memory than photographs. They can of course provide helpful backup.

'Lutradur', a synthetic material, was used for this piece to simulate the textures in the old decaying boat. It responds to heat and can be eroded away into lacelike shapes when exposed to the heat tool and so works well in this context.

Photograph by JL.

RED - 7

Selecting a subject to study

The Double Trouble philosophy has always been to encourage students to select a theme to research and study whether it is an inspirational subject or a technique in order to extend and maximise the design potential. Selecting 'RED' has certainly increased our own awareness.

The plant Anthurium, Flamingo Flower, shown on this page was a case in point. This species sports many variations, some with red leaves and greener fruit/flowers while others have green leaves and bright red flower heads. The many facets were intriguing to observe providing inspirational design options as the plant reached its zenith and then faded making some aspects appear more prominent. Using a magnifying glass, closer examination revealed colours and patterns not seen initially. These have been exaggerated in the samples shown. Each one illustrates the exploitation of one or two features. By simplifying and exaggerating the selected aspects and not attempting to copy nature, these observations provided a 'stepping stone' to the creation of some interesting designs.

Drawing of an Anthurium plant.

Aquarelle pencils, crayons, Koh-I Noor and gouache paints were used to record the growth changes observed.

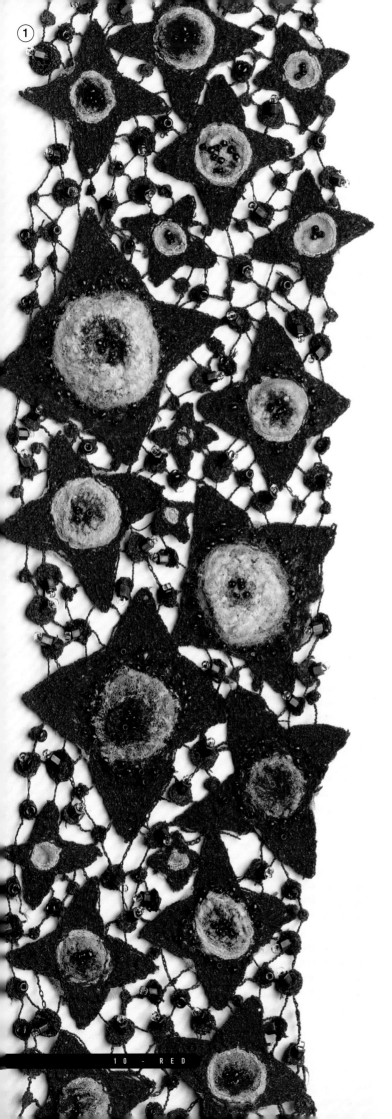

Aspects of the patterns observed on the previous pages were selected to exaggerate and feature.

1) This lacy piece was machined on a soluble fabric, 'Solusheet'. The drawing of the design was placed under the fabric in order to trace the lines to aid the stitching process. Small velvet and woollen fabric scraps were layered to form the centres of the main shapes and using the embellishing machine were fixed in place and moulded to protrude. Beads were stitched to the centres and to the smaller machined stitched circles.

2) This version of the design shows the bold shapes stitched in beautiful chunky silk yarns on a felt background material. The centres were treated using the embellishing machine as before in order to appear slightly dimensional. Beads were applied on top of free knot stitches to develop the texture further.

3) This stylised adaptation shows the main shapes as same sized larger repeating units. Red felt placed beneath a dark grey woollen cloth and other assorted fabrics applied on top were integrated by bedding with an embellishing machine. Straight stitches and beads suggest and highlight other aspects.

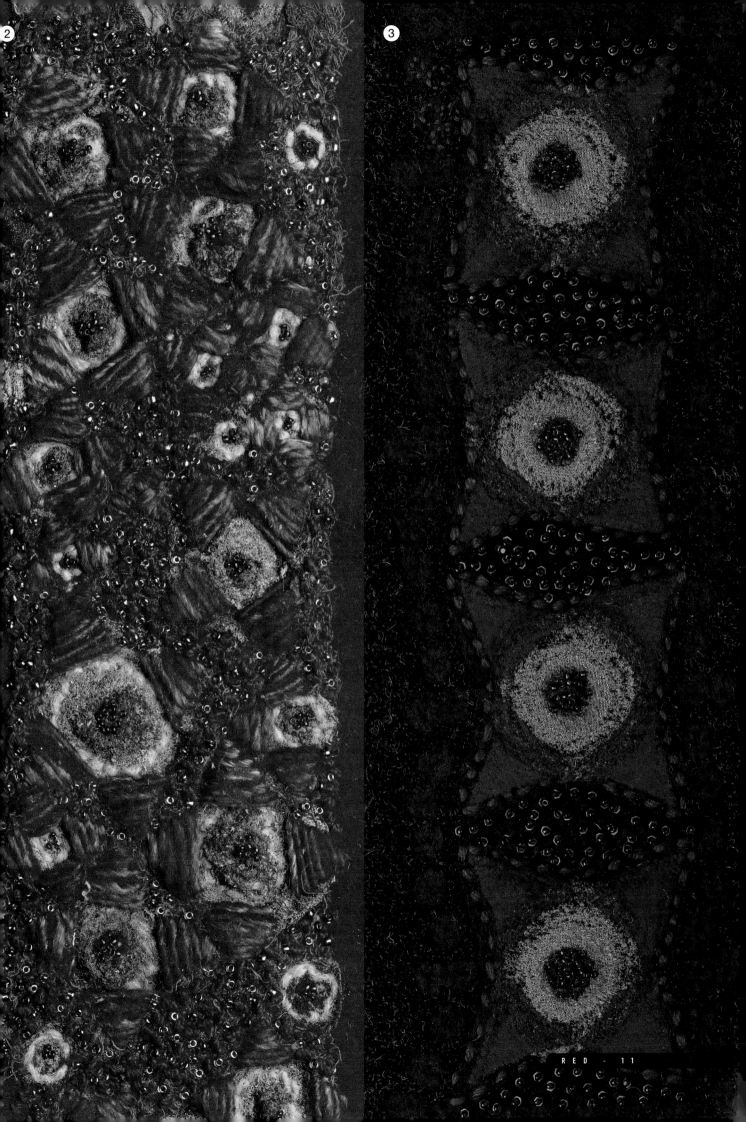

RED - 11

Red Centre - re-visited

The Red Centre in Australia is magnificent and continues to fascinate and inspire further work. Although red soil can be observed in Devon, Spain and other locations, it is the immense heat, historical significance and vast areas of space that continue to impress and seduce.

Whilst revisiting this area it was sad to see that fires had charred large areas of trees and scrubland. These appeared stark and contorted against the red earth. However, despite the rigours of the flames, new growth of bright blue green leaves could be seen at the base of many of the shrubs. These images of the complementary colours of orange reds and turquoise greens vibrating together were exciting to behold.

Pages from an Australian sketchbook recording

1) a range of patterns and colours of the diverse vegetation seen from the roadside.

2) the charred trees stark against the red soil with the beginnings of new growth.

3) Views from the air. Very quick diagrams with careful, comprehensive colour notes were made then developed in detail on reaching home.

The trial piece shown above was worked on a soluble fabric 'Solusheet' using layers of 'Lana' machine threads stitched in a variety of red hues. These were worked over a base of textured handstitches and wool and silk tops were applied to build up the soil areas. The contorted shrubs were textured with straight stitches worked in bold knitting yarns before these were gently machined to blend and integrate them within the whole work.

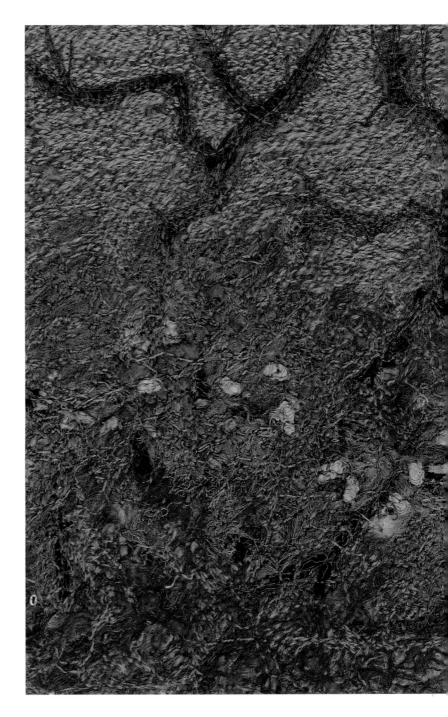

①

②

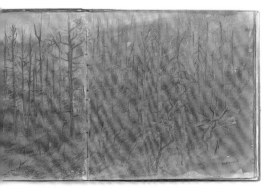

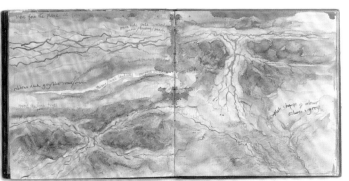

③

Reds in nature

Keeping a red sketchbook helps to focus observations and discover amazing reds in different objects and locations and the plant world is still one of the most inspiring sources of pattern, form and structure.

Red flowers attract attention as part of their drive for survival and the shades and hues are infinite. Petals take many shapes and configurations but the centres can be even more amazing. A close look with a magnifying glass will reveal the most remarkable shapes, surfaces and patterns. Taken out of context they become almost surreal and can inspire extravagant stitched and beaded surfaces as seen in the two samples shown on the opposite page.

Rich Reds

Reds can be rich or subtle, intense or delicate but in their strongest forms they are undoubtedly dynamic and have had great impact on many cultures.

Symbolically, red can represent power and love, and is the colour of life giving blood.

It is also associated with the 'forbidden', the colour of revolution and in many cases the devil. In India and China, red is traditionally the colour of marriage.

Various cultures, and most notably India, discovered red pigments in ancient times from ochers in soil and various plants such as madder.

Although we can gain inspiration from studying textiles from other traditions we should try to avoid 'cultural appropriation', or the mere copying of patterns from cultures other than our own. So many embroideries from India in particular have pattern upon pattern within their richly stitched surfaces and the set up illustrated here uses cloths that feature rich and dramatic reds. The South American San Blas Mola textile also shows marvellous red

patterns juxtaposed with greens, blues and blacks in strong dynamic patterns. These colourful textiles form the backdrop to voluptuous red tulips. Still life has traditionally proved an inspirational approach to drawing and design and can often be revisited with new slant.

One of the main advantages of a still life set up is that it can be done at home and drawn at convenient moments. The tulips will change and begin to flop but that can also be interesting and of course they can be replaced by fresh blooms or other red flowers such as roses or house plants. The purpose of

this set up is to find unusual and unexpected pattern and colour combinations rather than a literal still life composition.

The resulting studies exploit pattern and richness but in very different configurations.

There are numerous ways of working with still life groupings and the following suggestions may help to get you started if this is new to you.

Card viewfinders (assorted shapes cut out of card and held against the subject) are useful when isolating combinations of patterns, shapes and proportions.

Try small areas to start with and become familiar with the nature of the patterns and shapes. (For good still life exercises see Colour Explorations, Book 15).

Put in the basic shapes first and try not to be confused by details. It is also a good idea to think of one aspect at a time such as colour schemes, pattern or proportion and to work a series of quick sketches to aid the familiarisation process.

Try painting a section of the pattern directly with a broad brush to produce a free interpretation.

It is necessary to concentrate and not look up for the duration of the drawing to sustain the focus.

This approach is especially relevant to machine embroidery that often requires a continuous line for its successful execution.

When the drawing is complete it is interesting to find different aspects of the design by superimposing assorted paper windows such as slices, squares, rectangles etc.

The idea for 'a slice of life' came directly from this exercise by selecting a section of the composition and colouring it in. (see illustration left)

Once the studies have been worked they may be photocopied, traced, fed into computers and used for numerous developments involving different colour combinations, cutting up and reassembling, repeat patterns etc.

a slice of life

A quilting pen was used to draw in the main structure of the design onto the background fabric before carrying out free motion machine stitching.

The ground for this piece was an old damask tablecloth and the aim was to give the work a sense of drawing from the still life tradition.

Guided by the colour schemes a slice or section was filled in with free machine embroidery.

The completed machine stitching did not fully satisfy the intention but the use of the embellishing machine from the reverse of the work softened the lines and gave an almost pastel feel to the stitched line and better represented the idea behind the work.

Continuous line drawing

The exercise of continuous line drawing is one that many find liberating.

Select a pen or pencil and a piece of paper large enough to take the whole composition.

Before beginning, get comfortable, relax and take a few moments to decide where to start. Once the pen or pencil is on the page the object of the exercise is to work the entire drawing without removing the pencil or pen from the surface of the paper.

This will result in some rather interesting doubling up of lines and simplification.

a slice of life

Looking for Red

For centuries people throughout the world have known how to use red for impact.

The conventions of heraldry demanded that even from a distance flags and the trappings of war needed to be clearly visible and red was a major colour used in this way.

Today advertising exploits red to the full, drawing on both impact and symbolism to seduce and beguile.

Memorable images such as football stadiums awash with red scarves swaying to the chanting rhythms of the fans or fields of red poppies evoking poignant memories of the dead of world wars are etched into our visual memories.

However just a speck of red will have impact. Focussed looking will reveal less obvious sources of this powerful colour.

Above: *Photograph by JL.*

Left: *Detail from Shadow Paths, embellished mixed media.*

Take a dash of red

On a trip to Dover a red buoy gently bobbing up and down on the waves stood out clearly in a cool blue and green seascape, and necessarily so as it warned of danger. British beaches are often typified by gentle washes of yellows, ochres and greys and a fragment of red fishing net was visible from a considerable distance. This formed part of a group of red objects collected on a beach walk. On closer inspection some of the subtle shells and stones contained tiny seams and strands of pinks and dull reddish purples.

Just a speck of red in the landscape will demand the attention of the viewer.

In the dark days of winter crushed berries on a path will stand out against the frost and a lingering red leaf of autumn can be very evocative. The familiar red rubber bands, dropped by the postman on the pavement, sing out in the grey landscape.

Red roses have a strong place in poetry, prose and symbolism and when they fade they can decay into subtle and fragile forms. November gardens can seem muted but a closer look might reveal the last rose of summer fading but still clinging onto the bush.

A sketchbook that focuses on red will provide the inspiration for dynamic and subtle imagery and could be a lifelong study. It will certainly provide some surprising and unexpected combinations for pattern form and colour.

Warm and cold colours

When observing scenes of landscape and buildings and recording these by sketching or describing in words, notice how that in general the 'warmer' colours appear to come to the fore and 'colder' hues recede.

Many postcards sent from friends and relations will celebrate the various locations visited. These may include the highlands of Scotland or the fells of the Lake District.

In most cases it would be noticeable that the foreground of grassy hills is shown in 'warmer' tones of green, limes, olives mixed with a hint of red which contrast with the 'colder', paler blue and grey hues of the distant hills and mountains. Photographs of the Grand Canyon celebrate this fabulous wonder of the world where the strata shows an amazing range of reddish and ochre, warm hues but the distant ridges are tonally less distinctive and demonstrate a 'cooler' and greyer range of colour.

To demonstrate this point of view, the example shows a line of London's red buses in a busy street. Even if each bus had been painted with the same pot of paint, they would appear bright red in the foreground and paler and coloured in a 'colder' greyish red as the buses receded into the distance. By focusing on this aspect and re-looking at a collection of holiday snaps or digital images these observations will become more apparent. As always there are exceptions to every rule.

Primary colours always demand attention. A field of yellow sunflowers or buttercups show up to great effect as do the first stunning glimpse of luminous bluebells in the Spring. However, in most instances red usually is the centre of attention whether it be a warning flag on a beach, pots of scarlet geraniums, the Red Arrows flying through the skies at an air show or the breath taking sight of a field of poppies. In the past, a fashionable action taken by amateur photographers was to site their subject near a red object for greater effect. Warm colours can help promote a focal point within a panel where a viewer's eye can be taken on a journey toward the main area of interest. This is a useful suggestion as long as it is appropriate to the imagery and not too obvious. Careful thought should be undertaken for a subtle resolution.

In the natural world, the colour RED can attract and also warn or detract predators.

Welcome visitors to any garden are red and black spotted ladybirds or butterflies such as the Red Admiral with its distinctive red band across it wings. It is always joyful to behold the perky red- breasted British robin or in North America, the larger rose breasted robin or a flash of a Red Cardinal flying between the trees. It is interesting to note that the Cochineal beetle and the Madder plant have yielded red colour for our pigments and dyes.

Photograph by JB.

Photograph by JB.

However, some species such as the small, but lethal red backed spider and a tiny red frog (Poison Dart) are venomous and humans as well as others in the animal kingdom are extremely wary and warned to keep clear. Even the red spotted toadstools so often featured in Disney films or illustrated in children's books, although attractive to look at, are often poisonous. As a design source, many of the subjects mentioned could be an interesting challenge to study and the colour schemes, patterns and textures taken out of context could provide a fresh pathway to follow and lead to some exciting design developments.

Conclusion

The tranquillity of a sunrise can suggest peacefulness and hope for the day to come, whilst, viewing a sunset can evoke an emotional response regardless of how many times it has been seen. Photographs of spectacular red sunsets from all parts of the world are featured in travel brochures to allure and promote the location.

Over many years, these observations of amazing hues and changing colours have inspired artists such as Turner and Claude Monet. Writers and poets also wrote about sunsets and sunrise. Mahatma Ghandi wrote "When I admire the wonder of a sunset or the beauty of the moon, my soul expands in worship of the Creator".

Thomas Hardy wrote "Rays from the sunrise drew forth the buds and stretched them into long stalks, lifted up sap in noiseless streams, opened petals, and sucked out scents in invisible jets and breathings". Even more evocative are the words of William Shakespeare,
"As when the golden sun salutes the morn,
And having gilt the ocean with his beams"…

Often quoted is the saying 'red sky at night, shepherds delight - red sky in the morning, shepherds warning'. One can research myths, sayings and quotations that have been passed down through the generations. They could all spark fresh thoughts and new creative pathways.

By focusing on the colour RED it is hoped that your awareness of this colour will be sharpened so that new design ideas may be generated and that some of the facts, thoughts and symbolism mentioned may stimulate curiosity to research further. As well as general observations of this colour in everyday life, the colour red can stimulate emotional responses, which could lead to the creation of abstract interpretations.

As always, selecting a particular focus will give structure to your looking and provide 'stepping stones' towards a fresh approach to working with colour, pattern, texture and concept.

Suggested Reading

The Red Dyes-Cochineal, Madder, and Murex Purple - Gosta Sandberg - Lark Books ISBN 1-887374-17-5

Itten The Elements of Colour - Edited by Faber Birren - John Wiley & Sons, Inc. ISBN 0-471-28929-9

Colourful World - Armandine Guisez Galienne - Thames and Hudson ISBN 978-0-500-28586-2

Colour - Editor Helen Varley - Marshall Edition - ISBN 0-9507901-17

Colour - Victoria Finlay - Sceptre - ISBN 0-340-73329-2

Double Trouble

Booklets in this series include:
1 - Vanishing Act
2 - Voluptuous Velvet
3 - Bonding & Beyond
4 - Transfer to Transform
5 - Gardens & More
6 - Conversations with Constance
7 - Trees as a Theme
8 - Giving Pleasure
9 - New Dimensions
10 - Double Vision
11 - A Tale of Two Stitches
12 - A Sketch in Time
13 - No Stone Unturned
14 - Connections
15 - Colour Explorations
16 - Over the Line - Couching Rediscovered
17 - Grids to Stitch
18 - Seductive Surfaces
19 - RED
20 - Embellish & Enrich

Acknowledgments

Our thanks as always go to our husbands, Philip Littlejohn and Steve Udall who are so generous with their time and support in any endeavour we undertake. Sincere thanks go to Jason Horsburgh for continuing to design our booklets with such flair and to Michael Wicks for his superb photography.

The products and suppliers used in our books are listed at www.doubletrouble-ent.com

Photograph by JB.